"My mother said to me, 'If you are a soldier, you will become a general. If you are a monk, you will become the Pope.' Instead, I was a painter, and became Picasso."

For Coach ~ VL

100 Pablo Picassos

Special thanks to Violet's assistant, Paige Garrison,
a.k.a. "The Lifesaver," and Gray Fruisen for his lovely
drawings on page 4.

Designer: Beatriz Juarez
Copy Chief: Michele Suchomel-Casey
Concept and text: Mauricio Velázquez de León for duopress lab

First Edition

Paper ISBN: 9781938093326
ePub ISBN: 9781938093395
Kindle ISBN: 9781938093401

Library of Congress Control Number: 2014944121

Printed in China
1 2 3 4 5 6 7 8 9 10
duopress

www.duopressbooks.com

Scan this QR code
to learn more
about duopress

100

Pablo Picassos

Art by
Violet Lemay

duopress

This is **Pablo Picasso**, one of the most important artists of all time.

1

He was born in **Malaga**, a city in Spain.

Picasso's first word: "*piz*," short for *lápiz*, or pencil

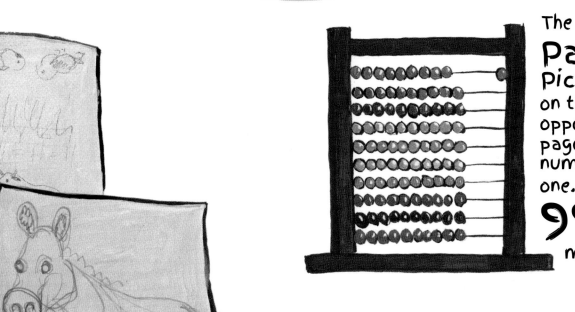

The young **Pablo** Picasso on the opposite page is number one. Find **99** more!

Pablo Picasso worked on all kinds of art; he was always busy and made more than **50,000** works of art in his life!

sculptures

drawings

Picasso made this sculpture, called *Bull's Head,* using pieces of an old bike.

Picasso designed costumes for a ballet company called **Ballets Russes,** in Paris.

costume designs

theater

Picasso was always happy to learn new things.

5

ceramics

He learned to make ceramics when he was 64 years old!

posters

collages

4

Picasso also wrote poems.

paintings

prints

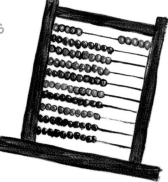

Sometimes Picasso was sad.
He painted many pictures
with the color blue.

6

This time in Picasso's
life is called his
Blue Period.

7

This is Picasso's friend
Carlos Casagemas.
When Casagemas
died Picasso was
really sad.

9

During the Blue Period, Picasso
chose to paint sad and poor people,
like this old, blind guitar player
he found on the streets of
Barcelona, Spain.

8

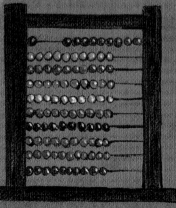

During the Blue Period, Picasso lived
in Barcelona and Paris. He stayed
in run-down apartments and
cheap hotels.

After the dark years of the Blue Period, Picasso found happiness. He changed the colors in his work.

Picasso was happy with the company of **Fernande Olivier**.

They met in Paris in 1904.

Fernande was not Picasso's only love. The artist had many girlfriends and wives. Picasso was always in love.

10

This time in picasso's life is called his
Rose period.

The Rose Period is named after Picasso's use of pink tones in his paintings.

Rose is the French word for pink.

12

11

In 1904, Picasso moved permanently to Paris. He made many friends who helped him to become a great artist.

Picasso and the painter Georges Braque worked side by side for many years.

Writer Gertrude Stein was a great supporter of Picasso.

14

Poets and writers like **Jean Cocteau** and **Max Jacob** were among Picasso's friends.

17

Henri Matisse was another great artist! Matisse and Picasso became very good friends... and rivals.

16

15

Picasso liked to paint himself.
He made many **self-portraits.**

Picasso painted
this picture of
himself when he
was 15 years old.

18

This is a picture
of Picasso, so you
have to count this
one, too.

19

20

A self-portrait
is a picture of you,
created by you!

Don't forget this Picasso!

22

Picasso liked African masks. These masks inspired him to paint people's faces in that style.

23

This looks like an African mask, but it's Picasso—so keep counting!

21

Another Picasso!

In 1907, Picasso completed a painting in a style that nobody had ever seen before.

Picasso made hundreds of sketches for this painting.

It was a big painting, called
Les Demoiselles d'Avignon.

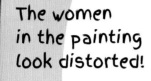

The women
in the painting
look distorted!

Two of the women's
faces remind us
of African masks.

The women don't look real!
That was shocking
at the time!

Picasso had
broken all
the rules.

In 1907, everybody
hated the painting!

Today, it is
considered a
masterpiece.

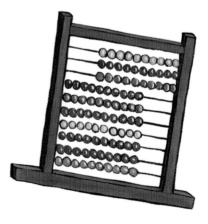

With *Les Demoiselles d'Avignon*
Picasso began a new art style called

CUBISM.

This picture is called
Three Musicians.

In Cubism, artists show all sides of an object in a single picture.

35

Georges Braque and Picasso worked together to create Cubist art.

38

36

Cubism made Picasso really famous!

Artists use Cubism in all kinds of mediums, from painting to sculpture.

37

Picasso loved animals, particularly **dogs!** He had many pets in his life, from a white mouse to a goat named Esmeralda.

Picasso's favorite dog was a dachshund named LUMP.

39

POUR LUMP
Picasso
September 19.4.57

He painted this plate for LUMP!

40

41

Gat

46

Yan

45

44

Esmeralda

42

Frika

43

From the time he was a kid, Pablo Picasso had always liked **bullfights.**

He also made many pictures of imaginary animals, like centaurs, fauns, and even the Minotaur!

The Minotaur is an imaginary beast that is half man and half bull.

52

51

Some people think that Picasso saw himself as the Minotaur.

In 1949, Picasso painted a beast using light!

He also made sculptures of these beasts.

50

49

In 1936, war broke out in Spain. One year later, the town of Guernica was bombed. Picasso was living in Paris, and he was very upset. He painted his most famous painting:

Guernica.

Guernica

Spain

57

58

56

Many people were
killed in the bombing.
Picasso showed this
horror in his painting.

Guernica is a huge
painting; it is bigger
than a professional
soccer goal.

Picasso used gray
tones to show the
sorrow of war.

War didn't stop in Guernica.
World War II started in 1939.

Picasso left Paris for the south of France.

In 1945, the war finally ended. After the war, Picasso made a simple drawing of a **dove.**

The drawing became a symbol of **peace** all over the world.

59

60

When Picasso was 9 years old, he made many drawings of birds.

Pablo Picasso had four children.
His daughter Paloma was born in 1949.
Paloma means "dove" in Spanish.

63

64

His other children were named
Paulo, Maya, and Claude.

61

62

After the war,
Picasso moved
again to the south
of France, where he
worked in sculpture
and ceramics.

Picasso worked in a cluttered studio.
He said that the messy room inspired him.

Picasso took an old
masterpiece called
Las Meninas,
by the painter
Diego Velázquez,
and made it his own.

Can you see LUMP
in the painting?

Picasso lived until he was 91 years old,
and he never stopped working.

76

museoPICASSOmálaga

75   74   73

Today, you can see Picasso's art
in museums all over the world.

He is a megastar
of the art world!

77

MUSEO PICASSO
PALACIO
BEREN MUR DE AGUILAR

86

78   79   MUSEU
Picasso

83

THE SCULPTURE OF
PICASSO

80

84

85

81   82

Picasso was very curious about the world.

He saw things differently and showed us the world in a special way!

Picasso's art broke many rules. He loved trying new ways to make art.

We saw

100

Pablo Picassos in this book.

Did you find them all?

87 88 89 90 91 92 93 94 95 96 97 98 99 100

Pablo Picasso was born on October 25, 1881, in Malaga, Spain, to María Picasso y López and Don Jose Ruiz y Blasco. His father was an art teacher. Pablo became interested in art when he was a little boy. In fact, Pablo's dad taught him art history and technique when he was very young; by the time Pablo turned 7, he was painting better than his own father!

The family moved to Barcelona and later to Madrid, the two largest cities in Spain, so Pablo could attend the best art schools in the country. At the age of 16, Pablo was enrolled in Madrid's Royal Academy of San Fernando. The teachers were impressed with his skills, but Pablo was not impressed with his teachers and skipped class a lot. Pablo didn't waste his time. He visited Madrid's museums often to see the paintings of some of the best Spanish artists of all time: Diego Velázquez, Francisco Goya, and El Greco.

In 1900, Picasso made his first trip to Paris, France. At that time, the best artists in the world were working in Paris. By 1904, he had moved permanently to Paris. He was poor and hungry, but he soon became a favorite of American art collectors Leo and Gertrude Stein. The Steins introduced Picasso to the French artist Henri Matisse. The two became lifelong friends.

Picasso painted one of his most important works—Les Demoiselles d'Avignon—in 1907. This painting started a new art movement known as Cubism. Picasso worked with painter and sculptor Georges Braque during these years and created many Cubist works.

Picasso painted another of his most famous works in 1937. The painting is called Guernica, after a town in Spain that was bombed during the Spanish Civil War. Guernica is a very large work that shows the pain and horrors of the war.

After World War II, Picasso moved to the south of France. By this time he was already one of the most famous artists in the world. But Picasso never stopped working and learning. He took on sculpture and ceramics and created many of his most beautiful works. Pablo Picasso died on April 8, 1973, in Mougins, France. He was 91 years old.

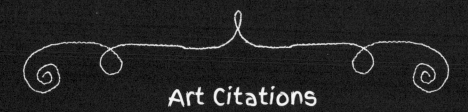

Art Citations

Illustrator Violet Lemay has respectfully interpreted the artistic styles of Pablo Picasso, the great artist to whom this book pays tribute.

All artwork cited clockwise from top. Page 4 *Pigeons*, 1890; *Bullfight and Pigeons*, 1890 (Various birds, donkeys, and bulls contributed by Gray Fruisen). p. 6 *Bull's Head*, 1942; *Le Chien*, 1936; *Costume for the Chinese conjurer in Parade*, 1917; set design for *Le Tricorne*, Ballets Russes, 1919. p. 7 *Owl*, 1951; *The Bull, state VII (Le Taureau)*, 1945; *Girl Before a Mirror*, 1932; *Violin with Sheet of Music*, 1912; *Valluris Exposition* poster, 1954. pp. 8-9 *Old Jew and a Boy* (or *Blind Beggar with a Boy*), 1903; *The Death of Casagemas*, 1901; *The Old Guitarist*, 1903. p. 11 *Circus*, 1915; *Acrobat and Young Harlequin*, 1905. p. 12 *Carafe, Jug, and Fruit Bowl*, 1909; *Musical Instruments*, 1908, by George Braque; *Portrait of Gertrude Stein*, 1906. p. 14 *Self-Portrait*, 1907 (African Period); *Self-Portrait with Short Hair*, 1896. p. 15 *Self-Portrait*, drawing, 1938; *Self-Portrait Facing Death*, 1972; *Self-Portrait with Palette*, 1906. pp. 16-17 Various studies for *Les Demoiselles d'Avignon*, 1906-1907; *Les Demoiselles d'Avignon*, 1907; *Head (Study for Les Demoiselles d'Avignon)*, 1906. p. 18 *The Three Musicians*, 1921. p. 19 *Portrait de Dora Maar*, 1937; *The Guitar Player*, 1910; *Guitar*, 1914. p. 20 *Pour Lump*, 1957. p. 22 top painting based on two works: *Bullfighting Scene (The Victims)*, 1901, and *La Corrida*, 1901; *Minotaur and Dead Mare Outside a Cave, with Young Veiled Girl*, 1936. p. 23 *Centaur*, 1955; *Picasso Paints Centaur with Light*, based on a photograph by Gjon Mili for *Life* magazine, 1949. pp. 24-25 *Guernica*, 1937. p. 26 *Dove*, 1949; *Pigeons*, 1890; *Hands Entwined III*, 1949. p. 27 *She-Goat*, 1950. Pages 28-29 contain many paintings and studies with the same title and date, including the two largest paintings shown on easels: *Las Meninas (After Velázquez)*, 1957. Also, above the mantlepiece from left to right: ceramic vase, date unknown; *Nature morte à l'aubergine (Still Life with Eggplant)*, 1946; *Four Faces*, or *Visage*, 1959. Additional works on page 28: *Still Life: Fruit Dish and Pitcher (Nature morte: Compotier et cruche)*, 1937; *Head of a Woman*, 1932; *Little Wood Owl*, 1949; ceramic plate, date unknown. Additional works on page 29: *Tête de Femme*, 1963; *Portrait of a Sitting Woman*, 1960; *Tête de Chèvre de Profil*, 1950; *Jacqueline with Flowers*, 1954. p. 30 *Visage No. 202*, 1963; *Woman in a Hat with Pompoms and a Printed Blouse*, 1962; *Woman*, 1961; *Buste de femme, les bras croises derriere la Tête*, or *Woman with Arms Crossed*, 1939; *Woman with Raised Arms*, 1936; *Jacqueline Sitting*, 1954; *Toro Bravo*, 1955. p. 31 *The Chicago Picasso*, or *The Picasso*, 1967; *The Kitchen*, 1948; *Suite de 180*, print on dress by White Stag, 1954. Back Cover *Man with Hat and Violin*, 1912; *Tête de Femme (Portrait de Françoise)*, 1946.

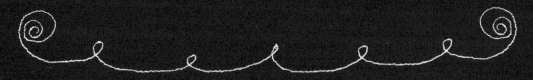

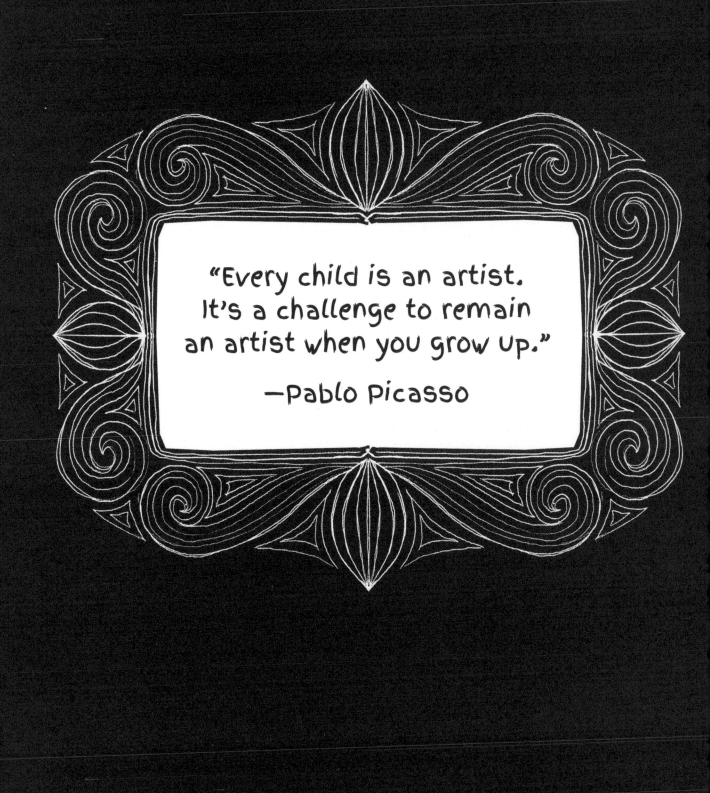

"Every child is an artist.
It's a challenge to remain
an artist when you grow up."

—Pablo Picasso